CW00482284

Robert Welch was born in Cork and educated there and at Leeds University. He is Dean of Arts at the University of Ulster. He has published poetry, fiction, criticism and drama. This is his fourth collection of poems. He is the author of a history of the Abbey Theatre, editor of the *Oxford Companion to Irish Literature* and his first play, *Protestants*, recently published by Lagan Press, was produced in 2004.

Also by the author

Poetry
Muskerry
Secret Societies
The Blue Formica Table

Fiction
The Kilcolman Notebook
Groundwork

Criticism
Irish Poetry from Moore to Yeats
A History of Verse Translation from Irish
Changing States: Transformations in Modern Irish Writing
The Abbey Theatre 1899-1999: Form and Pressure

As Editor
The Oxford Companion to Irish Literature
The Way Back: George Moore
Literature and the Art of Creation
(co-edited with Suheil Bushrui)
Selected Poems of Patrick Galvin
(co-edited with Greg Delanty)
W.B. Yeats: Writings on Irish Folklore, Legend and Myth
The Concise Companion to Irish Literature

Drama
Protestants

As Gaeilge
Tearmann

THE EVERGREEN ROAD

THE EVERGREEN ROAD

ROBERT WELCH

LAGAN PRESS
BELFAST
2006

Published by
Lagan Press
1A Bryson Street
Belfast BT5 4ES
e-mail: lagan-press@e-books.org.uk
web: lagan-press.org.uk

© Welch, Robert

The moral right of the author has been asserted.

ISBN: 1 904652 29 8 (pbk)
ISBN: 1 904652 30 1 (hbk)
Author: Welch, Robert
Title: Evergreen Road
2006

Design: December
Printed by J.H. Haynes, Sparkford

for Egan

Acknowledgements

Versions of these poems have appeared in *Cyphers*, *Poetry Ireland*, *The Irish Times*, *Southword* and the *Honest Ulsterman*.

The author wishes to express his gratitude to the following: John F. Deane, Wendy Taulbutt, Gerry McKenna, Christopher Ricks, Anthony Cronin, Brendan Kennelly, Máiréad Nic Craith, Ciaran Carson, Pearse Hutchinson, Patrick Galvin, James Hogan and Richard Bradford (the best reader of poetry I have encountered after Christopher Ricks!)

Contents

The Evergreen Road

The Revolver Sequence

The Evergreen Road

Five Meditations
for Hiroshi Suzuki

I

You are crossing
the mountains into
the next valley.
The summit is cloudy
with rain. Night falls
earlier now & wild
geese stir the cold air.
When you get to the city
think of me. As you drink
off the last mouthful
of fragrant soup lift
the bowl also
to my memory.

II

Dusk gathers
in the garden
of the Presentation
Convent. The Angelus
bell tolls; its last
chimes are prolonged
as the fragrance
of the roses deepens.

III

Pear-tree blossom
shades olive-green
branches on a still
day. Idling into
the warmth of the
stone-walled courtyard
a butterfly, radiant
& white. White flowers
exhale a frail
incense towards
powdery wings
trembling in flight.

IV

Three o'clock
of a Tuesday,
& it's raining
on the Evergreen
Road. The canopy
over Miss Ryan's
pharmacy is up
for the winter,
& Brother Dermot's
face is pale
beneath his umbrella
as he walks back
from the doctor.

V

We've pushed off
from the jetty,
my friends & I,
not forgetting rice-wine
& the round little
drinking bowls.
When I open the bottle
the smell of the wine
sharpens on the sea
breeze. The slow waves
are deep blue, & now,
look, the moon.

The Evening Echo

After the surgeon's dark consulting
rooms & the quiet exchange of
conversation, the walk down Summerhill
towards the grey semi-circle of the Coliseum
Cinema. Outside of which an *Echo* boy,
the great sheaf of newspapers clutched
in a brawny arm, was howling out
the paper's name, an impenetrable
& inscrutable phonetic shriek,
as he detached single copies to give
to passers-by, taking the coppers in
the selfsame hand. A few days
later the operating table was awash
with light, trees outside raked the sky
with green, as the surgeon turned away
from the washbasin, angled the tap closed
with his elbow, dried his hands, before
he pulled on the plastic gloves held
for him by a masked nurse. Huge windows
were open to the air as he cut through
to the knot of tension & accumulated
pus. The angry wound gave way
at last, while, in the fields beyond the city
midsummer wind coursed through the stands
of wheat; now & then there was, beneath
the susurrus of the shifting corn, a quiet
plosive hiss, as an ear of corn split open,
& white milk poured out from the husk.

Christt the King

The famously-fast Fr. Crowley
could do the Mass in twenty
minutes. From the consecration
on, his grey phizzog would flick
sideways to the clock every so often
to check his timing. Not even
his brevity could entice the hardchaws
who stayed outside in the porch,
or further away on the pavement,
smoking, eyeing up the fishnets
of Adrienne Corri in the *News
of the World*. Across the way
the sadness of the closed doors
of the Beer Garden. A tang
of stale porter smote the air
mixing with tobacco smoke,
the haze of sulphur off a blaz-
ing match. Inside, as the sun
clouded over, the yellow light
turned to umber, & Simon
of Cyrene bent down to lift
the cross off the shoulders of
the fallen Christ. Fr. Crowley
nodded a svelte head at
the tabernacle, genuflected swiftly
as from out the black chasuble
there popped, briefly, a black-
soled shoe, then swept off
to the sacristy. After which
a quiet but elaborate breakfast:
sausages, bacon, eggs, Old Tyme

Irish marmalade; soft toast
with the crusts sliced off; country
butter; lots of Barry's tea from thick
ceramic fired in Carrigaline.
On the jar of marmalade a black
cat sat before a blazing hearth.

The Legion of Mary: Mary Street
for Pearse Hutchinson

During the rosary we knelt
in a circle, facing out away
from each other, backs presented
to the empty centre. Each pair
of elbows rested on a chair-seat,
beads castanetting slightly
on the toughened ply as we felt
our way, bead by polished bead,
through the Glorious Mysteries.
Across the street, visible from our
vantage in the upper room, under a bare
electric light, the bald dome of
a shopkeeper, patiently sitting out
the intervals between his customers.
Above the cakes & sweets the yellow
tongue of a flypaper, stuck with swart
little carcasses. A long hand supported
his chin while a bony elbow
rested on the coarse grain of
the counter. We sang now of Her
who came as the morning, bright
as a host in battle array, while his
free hand turned the pages of *True Detective.*
There was the unmistakable, imperious
tattoo of stiletto heels on the sandstone
pavement, as, emerging from the dark
into the glare of a streetlight
a girl, with long red hair to her shoulders,
was revealed in the ferocity of her stride.
Her dress, a sheath of green energy,

shifted its folds & planes with the flex
& cut of the muscles in her legs.
Her face gave no expression as
her metallic clicks drove past
the huckster's shop, the bald pate
ignoring her, as she made towards
the Laurel Bar & the sailors there
from Gdañsk, Archangel, Leningrad.

The College of Christ the King: Capwell

The meniscus, boys—Brother Terence intoned
as he serenely expounded the concavity
water takes when it is confined.
He held the test-tube up and offered
a blue appraising eye to the transparency
and the tiny dancing bevel in the glass.
In the brown solemnity of the lab we
all felt the fierce tug of gravity,
the longing in everything to drag down towards
the fiery lodes at the centre of the earth.
I saw the galaxies as a huge meniscus
pulled down by that which brought them forth.

Turner's Cross: Midnight

The slide down Friars' Road
was deserted as we walked home.
A path of ice to skate on
at great speeds & sideways,
arms aloft to keep the balance.
A track of ice, inches thick,
made by pouring boiling water
from kettles carried from the kitchens
of the houses down the road,
plumes of steam disappearing
as the water hit the frozen tar.
The shining way stretched all before us
as we passed the Tangneys' shop
& Mrs. Lonergan's, which sold
sweets from bottle jars & snuff
in cones of twisted paper, as well as
cakes in trays from Madden's bakery.
In the silence I raised my gaze
& began to name the stars: Rigal,
Sirius, the Andromeda Galaxy,
letting on I knew the planets,
& my own one, the mighty Jupiter.
You stop & look at the moon,
letting the names fade from your mind.
It is so bright I can see the colour
of your maroon fur-lined boots,
the white grasses stiff behind
the privet hedges, the monkey-puzzle
throwing the stark geometry of its shadow
on the front wall of the McCarthys' house.
My hand is in the pocket of your
belted coat, &, as you move again,

I am pulled forward gently to where
our gate stands closed. I see
the concrete pathway to the door,
white between the neatly-
trimmed box hedging, kept
absolutely straight on all sides.

The Heat

You slow down in the night
when everything has become
hot with longing. Neither
knows what each is doing
as the grip loosens & then
you touch her flesh. You
sink down into the hidden
dark & you are trying
to do what is forbidden
and impossible. No one
has ever done this before;
you are breaking the last
rule in an agony of hope
that she will agree & not
stop you doing what you will
never forget. Now you don't
care that for years there
will never be any other colour
but iron-grey, that tint
of the aftermath staying
forever & only very slow-
ly fading from the light.
Your breath is sulphur
as you drop down further
into that entangled dark;
& what you're doing
is what will pull you
down to the deepest ring
of hottest Hell. Neither
knows which is which
as each yields more & more

to the other to satisfy
this craving that only
grows more ravenous
the more it's given in to.
Blindly you grope
towards the final opening.

The Wimple
for Peter Denman

Iron mesh across the schoolroom windows
qualified the light inside where rows
of kids, manic with fear, smelt
graphite & parquet polished with beeswax,
inhaled the chalk-dust & the body-heat
inside the bombazine. Sin was as present
as a slap across the face, rapid as a nun's rage.

One afternoon, the stink of congealed mutton fat
on my lips, I saw Sister Elizabeth
raise her left hand & point to the half-moon
of the wimple on her chest. Our souls,
after the first confession, would be white as that.
Then she spoke of the utter loss of pride
that will not yield, of the swoon of sin.

Later, she moved along the altar-rail,
pausing at each of our outstretched tongues,
to press them with a metal shoehorn, say
the words, then wipe the implement with a laundry towel.
Coming out into the sunlight I looked down Nicholas Hill,
saw the kerbstones cut from sandstone blue & shiny
with weather, & wanted to be something else:

a leaf on a tree above the limestone wall;
a blister on the red paintwork of the half-door
in the hovel across the street; the dirt on a girl's
bare foot going to the shop; the ping as the shop door
opens; the smell of comics, tea, & sausages;
the bakelite handle with which the blind is drawn;
the quiet half-light that remains.

The Evergreen Road: Kinsale Cottages

*'Pyramid O'Reilly could prove that the lost tribe of Israel lived
on the Evergreen Road.'*
—Patrick Galvin, *Song of a Poor Boy* (1990)

Unbeknown to anyone
my father has built me a crib
out of old timbers
under the pitch of the tin roof,
snug against the brick
of the chimney breast.

The air is warm up here
in the cold nights
of midwinter. Rain
whispers messages
as the wind separates
its voices over me.

I shall never be
so quiet again,
nor ever so still.

I know that everywhere
what is small & true
must go to ground, or
stow away in annexes,
immure itself in attics.

Late buses rumble past
the convent railings as,
one by one, yellow lights
go out in the shop windows
of the Evergreen Road.

Dark assumes the trays
of cakes, the boxes that contain
the penny bars. On the sidings
of the Bandon Railway
cattle trucks lie empty.

The chlorinated water
in the Swimming Baths
hardly stirs against
the white ceramic tiles.

Crosshaven

The corncrake's relaxed yakking
stroked the midday heat & went on and on
throughout the night; the corn
grew white under the moon but during
the day it moved, bright gold,
in the oven blast of the sun.

All around fields walled with stones,
white and bone-like in the heat,
& powdery to the touch. I lifted one
that sat exactly in my grip, drew back my arm
& threw the rock up high, then watched it
describe a perfect arc of fate.

My brother, in his thin white clothes,
stood below me looking away.
I shouted but it was too late. The stone
was falling through summer haze;
beneath it his slender neck, his hair.
I saw it strike then heard the darkened thud.

Church Bay

Noble Howlett was lying on his back
on the black shearing of sandstone
above the Men's Pool. Around him
a retinue of summer visitors & boys
from the row of council houses above
the bay. It was a Friday afternoon
with the heat rising from the rock
so when you looked up at the diver
standing on the outcrop way above,
he'd shimmer in the waves of air
before plunging to the olive depth beneath.
Conversation was in spurts, eddies, swears,
bravadoes, but everything quietened down
when someone asked the leader what it was
he'd had for dinner. Lunch was the word,
he said. Lunch. And, as a matter of fact
it was steak & kidney pie. Silence.
This is Friday, someone said. Howlett,
shifting languidly his brown legs in the heat,
turned over slightly further to expose a flank
already tanned, & said, well, the thing is,
you see, we don't fast in the church we go to.
We eat meat any day we want. Listeners
bowed their heads, or looked across to the stony
beach. One or two thought of cool interiors,
a pungent gravy. It was nice, he said.

Ballistics

for Lee Nolan

Incendiaries, we made gunpowder
in a shed out the back that smelt
of old bikes, rakes, lawnmowers
with perished rubber wheels.

The workbench was black with engine oil
& your granddad's cowrie knife hung
in its buckskin sheath above the door.
Boxes were stacked high with CALCUTTA stencilled

down the sides. We'd leave behind your grandma
in the warm dining-room & kitchen aromatic
with cardamom, fenugreek, & turmeric,
where she toiled away at her cottage industry.

Widowed, she made plaques of the Holy Family
by sticking blue & red & green transfers
on to snow-white ovals of plaster of Paris
baked solid in the oven also used for curries.

We, out the back, mixed charcoal pounded down
with sulphur flicked from off the tops of matches,
& saltpetre bought from pharmacists down town.
The shell we used was an old Electrolux attachment,

the snouted one you'd use for rooting into corners
on the stairway. We packed it with the powder,
bending the diagonal end back upon itself,
collapsing the other side in the benchvice jaw.

Carefully, then, we punctured the flank for the fuse.
We took it out to the garden, lit the phosphorus,
watched it fizzle, & waited as the mix took time
to take; then concussion, smoke, & a trail of flame.

Termonfeckin

A bamboo shivered.
Immense sunshine
& dry heat made
the long leaves whisper
& hiss as they peeled
away from the tough
green shoots of new
growth. A boy came
through an archway
set in the garden wall,
the pediments dark
with lichen. He
was carrying a gold
concert flute. The sunshine
caught the instrument
as he put it to his lips
to issue a single note
in the lower register,
dark in the full light.
He went back beneath
the lintel to leave
the garden open
to the bees, their different
sound, their hum.

Skehard: For Rachel

The morning you came into this world
I went down, at six a.m., to Twomey's shop
beside the Church of Christ the King, to buy
bread, milk, & the *Cork Examiner*. Behind
the counter, made up to the nines, even
at this hour, one of the ravishingly
beautiful Twomey sisters, famous for
their jet-black hair & sallow skin.
The bread man, in his light-brown overall,
reversed in the plate-glass door, pushing
with his back, his two arms holding the tray
of hot bread. He let the door close to
then turned about to face the counter
with a wink to me as he asked Miss Twomey,
most politely, if he could give her a selection
of Thompson's finest cakes. Oh yes, he could.
While he was out rootling between the metal
doors of the delivery van, I selected
a crusty duck*, hot from the tray, which she wrapped up
in a sheet of tissue specially kept for bread.

There was a fog and a light mist was falling
as I walked back up Skehard to the cross
where, above the railway line, not many years before
a knot of us would gather to talk of Elvis,
Shakespeare and (God help us all) the Greeks.
A fat lot we knew about any of these (or other)
topics. One time up here, it was a night in May,
I saw my music teacher, the best trombone-player
in the city, walking out with the girl who'd be
his wife & with whom he was soon going off to lay floortiles
in New York, New Jersey, & where J.J. Johnson
had, only recently, given up jazz to sell insurance.

And then, abruptly, your familiar: a little
puppy-dog, of a breed I do not recognise,
comes sidling towards me out of the fog.
Something odd about his gait; this tiny scrap
of being is managing to walk even though
his back is out of shape from some deformity.
It is as if Zeus, from the nuclear arsenals
stacked up on Olympus, has discharged a voltage
to hit a point exactly at the juncture of my ribcage.
This is the misfortune you've escaped; this small thing
is carrying what you might have been. What,
up there above the railway line, did we know
of the laws of pain, of the nature of disaster
not meant for us, but visited nonetheless?
I turn into the graceful curve of Capwell Avenue,
& see the light in the bare paned windows
of St. Finbarr's Hospital, behind one of which
your mother, scarcely more than a girl herself,
is looking, stupefied, into the wild blue eyes
you bring from wherever it was you came,
amongst the trackless spaces of the farthest stars.

*Cork term for a particular style of bread loaf

Adrigole

We are going to be here for less than a month
but already I've started to re-paint the walls
having scraped off the flaking paint & sought
out a tin of blue emulsion. On my desk I place
a bunch of wild honeysuckle, which fragrance
pulsates as I make the first of the revisions
of what is to become my life. Everything
is growing strange & lonely as I ready
myself for the plunge into famine, bad poetry,
the smell rising from the fields. Sometimes
it's as if I am on holiday, and I walk down
to the cross to take a pint, where, one evening
someone sings a song from the Borlin valley
that no-one understands. On a hot day
we drove up there to a bathing pool in the hills.
The granite burned beneath our naked skin,
but when we swam the water had the shock
of the subterranean. We clasped in its utter cold.

Leamagowra

The well has lain unused
for weeks, & the red ore
leached from the peat
has stained the water,
now harsh with the tang
of iron. Kneeling on
the step stone, I lean
down & plunge into
ochre depth the plastic
bucket until I scrape
bottom. Then I climb
beneath the capstone
to ladle up the last few
cupfuls off the blue clay
using the white enamel mug.

When I haul myself back out
the sun has lifted over
Crocknapeast & slashed
the frost-gripped heather
slopes of Slievetooey
with vermilion.

I go inside & light
the range, hoke out
the ashes of last night's
fire, & set the small
hard peats above the flame.
Four eggs to make an omelette,
milk, butter. When all
is ready I go to draw
water for the tea. Down

in the freshly rising depth
the blue till is clear,
every shard & stone
visible in the water
pulsing from its hidden
source. I dip the cup
& taste the mountain.

Crosshaven: Neptune Calms the Sea
adapted from Virgil's *Aeneid*, Book 1

It's off Roche's Point, and the sky is turbid & remorseless;
but even worse, with each vertiginous slide & hurtle
of waves that aren't waves but dark mountainous shiftings,
the warrior & his stricken sailors can see the actual sea-floor.
Neptune, at last, breaks surface, and thrusts his serene face
through the racing turbulence; he roars at Aeolus and tells him
to get the fuck back to Sicily & to keep his winds where
they belong, in the stones & caves that darken all that coast,
& to hold them there until the time comes when he is told
to let them out, by him, & not by anyone with scores to settle.
Even before he's finished shouting the sea quietens, the heaving
waves calm down, & the god, dispersing the thickened fog,
allows the sun to filter back, but slowly. And now Triton,
Neptune's son, and the sea-nymph, Cymothoe, push the ships off
jagged reefs, each one groaning as it thunders down,
Neptune steering them through the new-formed sandbanks
with his trident, always making sure
the water keeps as still as he has willed it to become.
Then, at last, the light wheels spinning cleanly, he guides
his chariot away across the surface of the sea towards America.

At Ballingeary

You'd gone ahead into the blaze
of green. The hawthorns were, as
in the early days of our marriage,
awash with white.

I recalled the lover in the song
who went out into the garden,
his heart breaking, to place his hand
on the blossoming tree.

A mass of yellow & yellow also
the primroses amidst which you kneeled
as you prayed
for what could never be attained:

that the woman at the roadside,
squatting next to a bucket of stones,
not fling them at the lorries, when they arrived,
carrying the killers of her only son.

The Feast of Lughnasa
in memory of Professor Barbara Hayley

In the house above the Foyle the doors
& windows are open to the air
off the estuary, scented with the smell
of meadowsweet as its tiny pollen
grains disperse in the sunshine.
The ivy clinging to the old stone
walls is interslung with strands of honey-
suckle. In the dining room a table
is set & decorated with late roses
& clusters of fuchsia gathered from
the hedgerows. Into the room, carrying
before her a dish of roast pork, her hair
loose, tanned arms bare to the shoulder,
comes Barbara Hayley, dead now for years.
The oak planks of the floor creak
as she leans across to place the salver
in the centre of the white damask.
The flowers, the fragrant smell of crackling,
mix with the air flowing in from the Lough
to create a welcome for the chief guest,
the man of honour & renown, who
has travelled all the way from Wicklow
to be here this day in his native Derry:
Seamus Heaney, walking up the slope
towards the house. He stands on the threshold
& Barbara's speech of welcome is in German,
two lines out of Göethe, eddying around
the word *Geist: Though the spirit is every-
where now reduced, it shines out still,
in English.* Seamus, smiling, bows his head.

Michael Hartnett in Alghero

The last time I saw him
he was gesticulating wildly,
in a narrow waistcoat
over a snow-white shirt
with billowing sleeves. This
was all happening on the sun-
terrace of the Calabona Hotel,
near the swimming-pool
& adjacent to the bar. He sang
arias to two Italian girls,
bowing to them between each phrase,
offering a style of Spanish or Neapolitan
courtesy, a Castiglione relaxation,
a *braggadocio* swagger, as
he swung his left arm behind him,
holding his right beneath his breast
to execute the perfect obeisance
to their tawny skin, their laughing
mouths, while, we others, not quite yet
in the final ranks of the great lord
Death, looked on, envious
of that *sprezzatura*, that *cortesia*.

In Piam Memoriam: Guy & Joel Harper

A son going down into a grave before a father: a thing not right in nature—what Harry Murphy said to me in the Cork Regional Hospital when his son, Tom, finally died from cancer of the colon after weeks of agony. *Contra naturam*, & *contra naturam*, also, the manner of Guy Harper's death & that of his father, Joel, less then two years after his son's. These must be remarked & set on record.

I

The iron grief of the father & the wracked
sorrow of the mother, as Joel shouldered
you out of the hushed church
where all that was audible was
the shuffle of the coffin-bearers' shoes.
His closed eyes near to yours,
the oak-boards in between, as he
carried you, stretched in the casket's satin,
on his back for the final time.

In the front pew, her body twisted in pain,
your mother gave you up to death as once
before she gave you up to life, not seeing
your shattered head, gazed upon
not less than a million times, which
she kissed first when you came into the world,
all blood, seeing then Joel's forehead,
that wide brow & jet-black hair,
registering the shock of a beauty
she could hardly bear, knowing well
it would draw down upon itself the anger
of the Gods, the malfeasances of
malicious men. No-one can be too special

in this rat pit of a hating world. None.
She knew that they would come looking for
you, & that you, with the courage
& ferocity of the man she loved,
carrying it in the very pulse that gave
you life, in the breath you took,
would not turn away, would take them on.

II

Sometimes the Fates do not remit their fury
until total suffering is achieved & it was she
whom they had chosen for the final test.
Some eighteen months had now gone past,
& she, strengthened by the fortitude
of a loving daughter, had hoped
the whirlwind of ungovernable tears,
remorse, & self-recrimination had begun
at last to subside when, once again,
there came the dreaded phone call
in the middle of the blackest night:
Was Joel O.K.? Was he back? We were off
on a small tear, the few of us, in Portrush,
& he said he'd take a turn before home.
Just making sure that all's well. That's all.

That was all. Beside her, where he should
be lying, the bed was empty. The frantic calls
began, the searches, the driving round
the deserted coastal roads till dawn.
Until, in the bleakest light of day
there was recovered the shattered body
of a man on the black basalt rocks
below Ramore Head, a place of sea
ravines, jagged outcrops, vertiginous falls.

III

Joel & Guy, serious artists of the barbecue,
when they carried in the dishes,
accompanied by ramekins of savoury chutney,
vast salads of greens & onions & tomatoes,
would each wear, as a kind of kitchen comedy,
tiny plastic aprons too small for their tall
& well-toned bodies, their monumental
energy, fearlessness, and strength.

Cuan Bhéil Inse: Valentia Harbour

When you come right down to the knuckle
what really matters is that semitonal
shift, the ground-base of all our woe
& expectation, the drift of waiting as one
note turns into the next. In that exhal-
ation, which is also suspiration, there's
the rattle of stones off a beach, the long wave
withdrawing; & you, perhaps, atop the escarp-
ment, looking down in bafflement at the house
you built from chalk-white fieldstone.

The Boy Zeus

The cave's vault plunges
to a dark seepage where
coins glimmer under
frowsty water. The square
of azure at the opening
only makes the sky seem
impossible & far.
Here, the child-god
sucked iron ore
from nipples of stone;
while above, in the brazen
sunshine, demons of air
and fire smote bronze
and screamed to drown
out the awful noise
of rock being ground
to pabulum by
the macerating jaws.
Kronos, the boy's father,
strode the skies,
letting loose downpours
of rain, jagged falls
of lightning, as
he searched for him
who'll work his overthrow.

A Shrine to Harpocrates
for Brian Friel

The floor is swept, the door
ajar; the threshold,
newly-washed, dries
in the sun, a slate grey
growing pale. A window
is open to the resinous air
off the pathways through
the pine forest. Between
the house & the trees
a clearing, into which
emerges from the shadows,
a man, a sheaf of cut
rushes on his back. In
the open warmth he moves
towards the house, where,
in an alcove, on a single
shelf, there stands a jar
of water, its level changing
slightly in the drifts
of air. Beside the jar's
cool depth, a stone.
A shelf of silence.

At Roaring Water Bay

The one you were going to
was a student of the law
& a master of language,
of the rhetoric that splits open
event to show the flaw
in the pourings of chance.

There is law & there is chance;
there is wild utterance.
There is longing & pain
knowing you will not come again.
Farewell, forever, to my angel,
& to forgiveness, too, farewell.

Mountsandel's Farewell
for Trevor & Julia, & Naomi

Orinoco's waters warm the cold sea
from Slea Head to Bloody Foreland.
The air is cold, smart with salt
over Tory, whose waves are falls
of green wash as night goes down
on Magheraroarty. A lone accordion
player strikes up in a pub on
the island. His low drone saddens
the air as the barman leans his elbows
on the counter to listen to the long
exhalations of loss. The note shifts,
a whistle climbs into solitary beauty:
they are playing a 'Farewell to Erin'.
Not too many listeners, a few
dispersed about the tacky bar;
the counter has an aluminium
edging, a plastic strip down its
centre, plywood panels stained an
oily varnish in 1953, formica
tables with surfaces clingy to
the touch. But music takes its place
whenever chance remits and opens
up a space for love to funnel through.

And here we sit, the departing chief
and I, and those whom we have chosen,
who, by luck's glad effort, also
have chosen us. Life is passing by:
oil tankers glide past the Azores
in mid-Atlantic; radars
of trawlers search the other radars
of the shoals beneath. Meanwhile men

agitate their bile-ducts in Committee
Room B; a young girl lifts a stocking
from the back of a chair in a hotel
in North London; while we, we share
an old bottle of Nicolas Vieux Ceps
over the dingy table, as, now, the piper
growls out 'The Waves of Tory' before
he returns, once more, to the exile's lament.
And now I turn to you, your laughing face,
and say that now, far from being a stranger
to us, you are becoming an exile, through
your force of love, your wariness, your
watchful effort, but mostly, mostly, love.

Mo Ghile Mear
for Charles J Haughey

There is an excitation of light
outside the window. Two brown shapes
move across the field of vision, a doe
& her leveret. Miles away, in Dublin,
at the periphery of declining power
you sift through pages you've already
riffled, ceaselessly, turn once more
to the columns of figures, hoping your
watchfulness will see you through.
In chamber after chamber you discover
livid faces cowled in hate. You calm
your breath, still your wild heart.
Through the long wet grasses the hares
have trampled a pathway to the wire
fence, underneath which they've made
a grassy torc, braided with clover
& with buttercup: their getaway.

The Revolver Sequence

1

The Typewriter

That was the day, you recall,
when, mastered by the remorseless
urgings of what was becoming inevitable
(knowing there was to be no respite
from the ferocious & calm accumulation
of those non-transferable surcharges
on our lives) I walked down the precinct
to buy, probably, the last, the very last
manual typewriter ever to be bought in Coleraine.
It was for you to write your stories on,
the ones about the sea, the small child lost
& you finding him again against all odds.

Surcharge

'In sum, it would appear, Professor,
that your reach once again
has exceeded your grasp.'

This is taking place in an upstairs room
in a bank overlooking the Diamond,
a place for storing files, dead letters, old mortgages.

I'm looking at the manager of amortisements,
seizures, entails, surcharges, & thinking
what his life is like out in Bushmills

& for no other reason than that he's used
the word 'grasp'.
I see my father's laughing face saying:

'That's what I did with the little bastard;
when he said that I threw him out by the hasp
of his arse.'

3

A Life in Bushmills

When you boil it right down
to the absolute elixir, the shimmering
whiteness of a ghostly ectoplasm
of an essential trace of a tint
of a hint you get:

slowdown; warmth of an April
evening with the sun deepening
the old ochre paint of a bench
beneath the basalt clock tower;
the plainness of the cenotaph;
the brilliant colours
of the Union Jack.

& just as soon as said,
it's dead
& gone, as far away as fifties Cork,
listening to the radio in a terraced house
up Friars' Walk, the biscuit tin of lead
soldiers under the sideboard,
a photograph of Nadja Tiller
in a copy of *Men Only* in the bookcase
in the front room, waiting to be looked at.
She's in black & white, & she's wearing a slip,
in a still from a film called *The Rough and the Smooth*.

Maybe it's smooth in Antrim.
That is what Carlos Santana might say.

Listening to the Radio

We got tuned in after rippling through the static
by twiddling the fluent bakelite knob
on its mitred edges. It slid so easily past
Hilversum, Dublin, to find Athlone,
the frequency to pick the signal up all
the way from Philadelphia.

                  The Rocky Marciano
title fight against Jersey Joe Walcott,
at two o'clock in the morning; my father up
even though he's got the early shift in the morning;
Tom & Jim & Sonny all there as well; Gold Flake
being lit & smoked, the whole kitchen a haze of blue,
acrid & aromatic. When Marciano went down
my grandfather, Michael Kearney, clenched his fist
& said: 'Get up, get up', his blind eyes closed
against defeat.

               'He's way behind on points,'
he said, when, out of nowhere, Rocky finds the punch
that knocks out Jersey Joe in the thirteenth round.

'California, here I come,' said Michael Kearney,
picking off the butt stuck to his lip,
& outing it, as he always did, by rolling the lit stub,
almost caressingly, between his black & yellow palms.

'Right back where I started from,' my father says.

The Kit Bag

On the Railway Road I met Johnny J.,
someone I hadn't seen for a while
& not much at all since his removal
to the serenities of Culdaff in Donegal.
Soon we came round to the topic he knows
a thing or two about (he's in insurance),
& that's trouble.

    'There's always someone
much worse off than yourself, no matter what.
I met this boy a while back who said
if you threw all your troubles into a corner,
then asked everyone else to throw theirs in on top,
& started sifting through the lot to find your own
again, you'd be glad to have them back once you saw
the shit everyone else has to put up with;
& that's a fact.'

    Johnny J. said this to me
in front of the cash dispenser on the Railway Road.
So, pack up your troubles in your old kit bag,
& though there may yet be a long while
to go before dark (& yet there may not),
might as well pack them up & smile, boy, smile.

Inveterately Convolved

Across the street from the church
there lived the moneylender, Nora O'Dwyer;
her little house was painted turquoise,
& had small windows of thick glass
always kept spotlessly clean. At Mass
on winter mornings she wore a headscarf
with an equestrian motif & maroon
gumboots, fleece-lined, with the tops turned down.

At the corner of Maiville Terrace was
the fish & chip shop where I'd be sent,
some nights, for a late supper of battered sausages,
chips, a fish; which I'd carry home, warm,
in its three-times-wrapped cocoon of newsprint,
the heat evolving to my side & arm.

To be then unwrapped in the intense fluorescent
of the newly-extended kitchen, with, maybe,
Miss O'Dwyer up after the Miraculous Medal,
Mrs. Barrett in from Ballyphehane. The astringent
smell of vinegar would hit the air, the fish
would be divided in its crunchy casing, the chips
apportioned out on plates warmed up, especially.

For Saint John's Eve a heap would be made
on the waste ground over-right the chip shop
of everything that could be found that would burn:
mattresses, old cots, armchairs with the stuffing
hanging out, rubber tyres, great bates of wood,
worm-infested rafters; there they would be,
in the accumulating mound, inveterately convolved

in the lonely sunshine or the solemn brightness
of June days overcast with cloud.

Once, on such a day of midsummer gloom
& opportunistic gathering for the bonfire,
I found myself alone inside the grounds
of our closed-up school, someone having left
the heavy iron-grey gates wide open.
Beside the gravelled drive a grassy verge
on which was planted, at regular intervals,
a stand of palm trees close along the wall
of pebbledash, making a covert tunnel
of scented darkness running upwards,
a hidden alternative to the open way.

I entered at the bottom & found myself
involved in aromatic shade as I strove
upwards, pushing by the snappy branches
& crouching down to negotiate the thicker limbs
& softer fronds. On my right the rough surface
of the wall, once painted white, now darkened
by the brown umbrageous light & inner must
of the difficult passageway between the concrete
& the palms. Underfoot a deep & silent mast
of kernels & of withered branches on which
no other herbage could find nutrient for growth.
I pushed up, taking small lacerations on my face,
until I reached the driveway top, all the while
aware that no-one could remark that darkened progress.

When I came out the gates still stood open.
Mr O'Mahony, in his butcher shop, was attending to
a late afternoon customer, & the 3A bus
was navigating the corner of the Lower Friars' Road.

Revolver

Tomás MacCurtain, it was said, just took it out
& shot a member of the Free State Special Branch
dead in broad daylight on King (now MacCurtain) Street.

When my father told this story I'd get the smell
of holster leather, gun-oil, a levelled gaze
of blue eyes under a shock of white hair.

All of this takes place under the serene slant
of the spire of the Presbyterian church. Its Sunday School
classroom is used, from time to time, for rehearsal,

by the trombone section of the Barrack Street Band.
The *glissandi* of the opening bars of the *Belphegor March*
can be heard down as far as the Brian Boru Bridge.

A kind of fanfare to the drawing apart of the twin
cantilevers of the bridge, as, battleship-grey
machinery revolving, the two halves are lifted up.

New York

The boat in which she took me
away across the dark narrows of the inlet
was of straw, the prow gathered
to a knot of burnished tension,
like a corn dolly,
or the crest which might surmount
a mummer's headgear. She lit a match
& sulphur flared to crimson in the sea-wind
briefly, before it all reverted
back again to Cimmerian gloom.

Or that was what the teacher called it
back in Strangford as he taught us how
to strip the pith of rushes to make tapers
for the lamp.

        Now the light craft swung
between the shifts of waves until I heard
the soft swish of the prow against a face
of rock or stone. Suddenly the light flared up
once more & above us in the boat I saw
Liberty raising her adamantine torch
over flotillas of liners, merchant ships,
destroyers, tenders, dredgers, each one
following a course, each one followed by
a wave of creamy light.

                I see
that in this main of action she's the one
I saw below Poyntz Pass one night in May
in a drinking den beneath the town
after a gang of us had shagged ourselves
saving barleycorn for days on end.